Explorers of the Land

by Jeff Putnam

Explorers of the Land
by Jeff Putnam

Illustrations by Michael DiGiorgio

Photography: p. 2 © Digital Image © 1996 CORBIS; Original image courtesy of NASA/CORBIS; p. 3 © Gianni Dagli Orti/CORBIS; p. 6 © Dallas and John Heaton/CORBIS; p. 12 © Roman Soumar/CORBIS; p. 14 © Bettmann/CORBIS; p. 15 © Michael S. Yamashita/CORBIS; p. 18 © Arne Hodalic/CORBIS; p. 27 © Historical Picture Archive/CORBIS; p. 30 © Jim Zuckerman/CORBIS; p. 31 © Staffan Widstrand/CORBIS; p. 35 © Kevin Schafer/CORBIS; p. 38 © Bettmann/CORBIS; p. 42 © Lee Snider/CORBIS; p. 44 © Craig Tuttle/CORBIS; p. 47 © Peter Harholdt/CORBIS; p. 52 © Bettmann/CORBIS; p. 56 © Bettmann/CORBIS; p. 64 © L. Clarke/CORBIS; p. 70 © Nik Wheeler/CORBIS; p. 74 © Bettmann/CORBIS; p. 80 © Bettmann/CORBIS; p. 81 © Bettmann/CORBIS; p. 85 © Roger Ressmeyer/ CORBIS

Nonfiction Reviewer
John Barell, Ed.D.
Educational Consultant
The American Museum of Natural History
New York City

Art Buying by Inkwell Publishing Solutions, Inc., New York City
Cover Design by Inkwell Publishing Solutions Inc., New York City

ISBN: 0-7367-1797-8

Web sites have been carefully researched for accuracy, content, and appropriateness. However, Web sites are subject to change. Internet usage should always be monitored.

Zaner-Bloser, Inc., P.O. Box 16764, Columbus, Ohio 43216-6764, 1-800-421-3018

Printed in China

04 05 06 07 (321) 5 4 3 2

Table of Contents

Introduction

Have you ever heard the song, *"The Bear Went Over the Mountain"*? If you have, then you know why that famous bear went wandering all over. He just wanted "to see what he could see" on the other side of the mountain!

In this book, you'll read about many different explorers, some famous, some not so famous. All of them, however, have something in common with the bear in the song. These men and women traveled all over the face of the earth, just to see what was out there.

You'll learn about how these explorers crossed blazing deserts, scaled the world's highest mountains, and navigated the most treacherous rivers. They suffered extreme heat as well as finger-numbing cold. They battled wild animals and deadly diseases. They had to make peace with people they met—or pay a harsh price.

What drove these people to risk their lives traveling into unexplored lands? For many of these brave men and women, there was a desire to be first. They wanted to go where no one had ever gone before or to do something no one else had ever done.

Many of the people you'll meet did not survive their journeys to explore unknown parts of our Earth. Some even rest in unmarked graves far from their homes. Others returned to fantastic welcomes. All of these explorers took their places in history.

The explorers in this book come from many different cultures and time periods. You'll read about a Chinese Buddhist monk whose love for travel led him over mountains and deserts in search of knowledge. You'll learn about a Muslim who explored the world of Islam from

1

Arabia to Timbuktu. You'll encounter the brave men and women who first unveiled the secrets of Africa, North America, South America, and Australia. You will also read about the thrilling attempts to explore the world's great mountains and the deadly wastelands at the South Pole.

You'll find out about the special challenges explorers of the earth face today. Technology has made our world more accessible, and its unexplored places are becoming fewer. You will learn how explorers of our time are often scientists. They go on their journeys of exploration in hopes of solving the serious problems we now face. How can we preserve fragile environments and **habitats**? How can we help at-risk animals and plants to survive? Can we find new ways to grow food and create homes for the earth's ever-increasing population?

When you finish this book, you may be able to answer the ancient question: Why do people go exploring? You will definitely find out who the explorers of the earth were, when they lived, why they traveled, where they went, and what they were looking for!

The final chapter looks at the future of Earth exploration. Believe it or not, there are still corners of our planet where no human has ever been! Where are some of these mysterious places, and why have they remained unvisited for so long? How long will it be until even these hidden places are finally explored?

Chapter 1

Our Earth

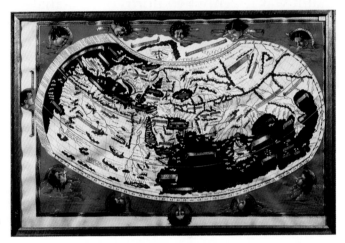

When we look at a globe or world map, we take for granted that what we are seeing is accurate. Thanks to technology like *satellites* that can take pictures from outer space, we now have a very accurate picture of our world's geography. But it wasn't that easy for the early explorers.

A man named *Claudius Ptolemy* (**klaw•dee•uhs tol•uh•mee**) was a Greek scholar who lived between A.D. 127 and 147. He decided to make a more accurate map of Earth. His map listed grid positions for about 8,000 places. The map was very detailed, and scholars and mapmakers from other parts of the world were anxious to copy it. Throughout the centuries, many explorers used the map.

Unfortunately, there was no way for Ptolemy to measure distance accurately. Consequently, many of his grid positions were wrong. As explorers began to venture out beyond their own countries, they realized that not only were positions of the places wrong, but the whole map was wrong! Ptolemy had no idea how big Earth was. He believed that it was roughly two thirds of its actual size. Ptolemy's map did not even include North America and South America! As you will see, that created a big problem for some European explorers.

Today we know that Earth has seven **continents**. Can you name them? They are North America, South America, Africa, Asia, Europe, Australia, and Antarctica.

The Seven Continents

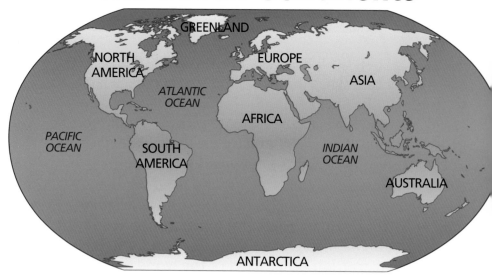

GREENLAND

NORTH AMERICA

EUROPE

ASIA

ATLANTIC OCEAN

AFRICA

PACIFIC OCEAN

SOUTH AMERICA

INDIAN OCEAN

AUSTRALIA

ANTARCTICA

The seven continents are scattered around the globe and divided by three major oceans. What are their names? If you answered the Atlantic, Pacific, and Indian, you're right. There are also many other smaller seas around the world, such as the Caribbean, Mediterranean, and Arctic. A small amount of Earth's land area is contained in islands. Do you know the world's largest island? It's Greenland, which lies in the North Atlantic Ocean.

Location was not the only thing that concerned explorers. The land areas of our planet have incredible variety. How many different kinds of land areas can you name? Here's a starter list. You may be able to add suggestions of your own to this starter list: mountains, forests, deserts, plains, swamps, coasts, and jungles.

All of these different kinds of land areas have been explored over the years. Some are easy to get to, like plains and coasts. Others, like mountains, deserts, jungles, and polar regions, are a lot harder to reach. It's not surprising that the easy places were explored first. The hard ones came later, sometimes a lot later. One of the last unexplored places on Earth is the jungle region around the great Amazon River in South America.

Read on to learn about these amazing journeys and the courageous adventurers for yourself! Each of these places presents its own special challenges to explorers.

Chapter 2

Across Asia

I t's difficult to say who the very first explorers were. Most historians think that real explorers are those who set out to make a discovery, to see new lands or the people who live in them.

China's Route to the West

One of the world's oldest civilizations, China, was one of the first to explore the world that lay outside its borders. The journeys of the explorer Chang Ch'ien (chahng chyehn) tell us a lot about why people began to explore.

When Wu-Ti (woo-dee) became emperor of China in 140 B.C., the country was threatened by a group of barbarians known as the Huns. From time to time, the Huns raided the borders of China causing havoc and destruction. The Chinese built a barricade called the *Great Wall* to protect themselves from attack, but it wasn't enough. In 138 B.C., the Chinese emperor asked one of his officials to travel across land to the home of a **nomadic** people called the *Yueh-chih*. Why? The emperor wanted to make a military alliance with the Yueh-chih against the fierce Huns, who lived to the north and west of China.

Chang Ch'ien set out in 138 B.C. with about 100 men. To show that he was on a special mission for the emperor, he carried a special object—a black yak's tail! As soon as Chang Ch'ien entered the Hun's lands, he and his men were taken captive. They were held there for 10 years. During this time, he was married and had a son. When they finally managed to escape, they went on in search of the Yueh-chih. By the time they reached the Yeuh-chih people, they had abandoned their nomadic life and they were not interested in fighting the Huns. Chang Ch'ien and his group stayed with the Yeuh-chih for a year, and in 126 B.C. they began their long journey home.

This time, hoping to avoid being captured, the explorers decided to take a southern route. Yet, once again they were captured and held prisoner for almost a year. After finally gaining his freedom, Chang Ch'ien explored as far west as the Khyber (**keye•buhr**) Pass. The pass lies between India and Afghanistan (af•**gan**•i•stan) today. On his way back to China he traveled through the mysterious land of Tibet (ti•**bet**), high in the Himalaya (him•uh•**lay**•uh) Mountains. This trip lasted 13 years. When he returned, only one man out of the original hundred came back with him.

Chang Ch'ien returned to Wu-Ti's court with his wife and son. His original mission had not been accomplished. However, he had learned a great deal during his travels. He was the first person in China to travel west beyond the Chinese borders. He told the emperor about the rich civilizations of Rome and India. The explorer knew that trade with these distant lands could make China rich.

The information Chang Ch'ien brought back fired the imaginations of many people. And Wu-Ti was impressed with the prospect of trade. Seven years later, the emperor sent Chang Ch'ien on another journey. On this second mission, he traveled into what is now Kazakhstan (kuh•**zahk**•stahn). From here, Chang Ch'ien sent assistants to explore in Uzbekistan (uz•**bek**•i•stan) and Afghanistan. He and his assistants collected as much information as they could about the lands they visited. The contacts Chang Ch'ien made helped the Chinese trade with cities founded by the Greek general, Alexander the Great. This contact led to the spread of new ideas as well as new products, such as grapes and better horse breeds. Today, Chang Ch'ien is considered by many historians to be the Father of the Silk Road, a trading route between China and the West.

The Silk Road

Chang Ch'ien's travels helped lay the foundation for one of the most famous trading routes in history—the Silk Road. The name is a little confusing because it wasn't a single road. The *Silk Road* is the name used for the trading routes between China and Europe. It was the main trade route from about 100 B.C. until sea routes opened more than 1,000 years later. One of the most important things that China had to trade with the western world was an incredibly beautiful, smooth, thin cloth called *silk*.

The trading route was over 4,000 miles long and ran from Xi'an (**shee•ahn**), China, to Roman ports on the Mediterranean Sea. **Caravans**, or large groups of merchants and their goods, set out westward on camels. The caravans were loaded with spices, rare woods, jewels, pearls, silk, and

Did You Know?

During his travels, Chang Ch'ien ran across many things that fascinated him. About 2000 miles from the court of Wu-Ti, Ch'ien discovered a breed of horses that were thought to sweat blood. They possessed amazing qualities of size, stamina, and strength. Since the campaigns against the Huns demanded strong horses, Wu-Ti was delighted when he heard about them. He named them *Celestial Horses* and brought them back to his court. Since then, the Celestial Horses have been bred in China. They became a status symbol for rich men and government officials.

Why did these horses sweat blood? It remained a mystery until recently. Apparently, it was caused by a parasite that burrowed under the horse's skin. It produced small swellings that burst and bled. Silk Road travelers in the nineteenth and twentieth centuries have also recorded this phenomenon with other breeds of horses.

even some fragile porcelain pottery. These valuable goods would be traded to merchants from Mediterranean countries for gold, silver, wool, and horses. Because the route was so long, traders did not travel the full length of the road. They traveled to trading posts along the route where they exchanged their goods with other merchants. It was almost like a relay.

The Silk Road wound its way through deserts and over mountain passes. In spite of these hardships, the greatest danger came from bandits. Groups of nomads attacked the caravans, killing the merchants and taking their goods. At its western end, the Silk Road met the Mediterranean shore. From there, goods were carried by ship to Greece, Rome, and other countries.

The Silk Road

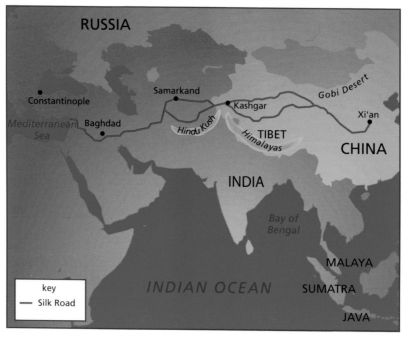

In Search of Buddha

Over time, silk, spices, and gold were not the only things that traveled along the Silk Road. Ideas also made the journey from civilization to civilization. The central Asian regions along the trade route learned about Christianity, while Buddhists (boo•dists) from India took their religion to China.

About 700 years after Chang Ch'ien, a studious young man named Hsuan-tsang (shoo•ahn-tsahng) became fascinated with the Buddhist religion. **Buddhism** teaches that by living right and doing good, one is freed from pain, sorrow, and desires. He became a Buddhist priest at a young age, but he was still not satisfied. The young man decided that he wanted to learn more about the interesting religion. The Chinese translations of Buddhist writings were incomplete, and this troubled him greatly. Even his Chinese teachers could not answer his questions. It was against the law to leave China in A.D. 629, but Hsuan-tsang decided he must take the risk. He decided to travel to India and bring back more books so that the Chinese translations could be complete.

Hsuan-tsang traveled from A.D. 627–643. He traveled along the Silk Road west toward India. First, he crossed the Gobi (goh•bee) Desert of northern China and Mongolia (mong•goh•lee•uh). He continued west and then turned south and traveled over the awesome mountains of the Hindu Kush (hin•doo kush) into Kashmir (kash•meer) and northern India. Along the way, he stopped to study at Buddhist monasteries. His goal was the home of Buddhism in eastern India. During his travels, Hsuan-tsang studied Buddhism and collected its writings.

In 643, Hsuan-tsang decided it was time to return home to China. Hsuan-tsang took with him 520 boxes of Buddhist writings, which he planned to translate into Chinese. On the trip, he lost much of his baggage, including some rare flower seeds, in a river accident.

When he finally arrived at the emperor's court, after 16 long years of traveling, he received a hero's welcome. Instead of being angry that Hsuan-tsang had broken the law by leaving China, the emperor was fascinated by his amazing stories of life in other lands. He gave Hsuan-tsang many gifts and offered him an important job at court. The weary traveler refused.

Hsuan-tsang wanted to spend his time translating the Buddhist writings he had brought from India. By the end of his life, Hsuan-tsang had translated 73 texts he had brought back from his journey. Even though he refused the offer of the emperor, he wrote a popular book about his travels, *Records of the Western Regions*. When the great explorer died, he was a hero. The emperor cancelled all official business for three days.

Statue of Buddha in India

Marco Polo

Remember the Silk Road? It was so long and dangerous that the people only traveled on portions of the route, exchanging goods at trading posts. However, in 1271 two Italian brothers traveled the entire Silk Road, from west to east. One brother's teenaged son joined them. Their journey made the boy the most famous land explorer in the world. Do you know what his name was?

Venice, Italy, was Europe's leading trading city in the 1200s. The city's location in the eastern Mediterranean Sea made it a good starting point for goods headed to the East. Goods from the East were often unloaded in the city's harbors. In the year 1271, the boy began a journey east with his father and uncle. His name was Marco Polo. The book he would someday write about his travels across Asia made him world famous.

Nicolo and Maffeo Polo were merchants in Venice. They had business arrangements with the *Mongols,* the nomadic people who had conquered China in the early 1200s. The young boy Marco and his father and uncle were to travel to the court of the Mongol emperor of China, Kublai Khan (**koo•**bluh **kahn**). They set sail from Venice to Constantinople (kon•stan•tuh•**noh**•puhl), today known as Istanbul, Turkey. Then they traveled by caravan through the desert to Baghdad (**bag•**dad) and then to the port city of Hormuz (**hor•**muz). At Hormuz, they decided it was too dangerous to try to sail to China. Instead, they headed for the Silk Road.

The Polos crossed the mountains of the mighty Hindu Kush and joined the Silk Road. All along the way, the young Marco paid careful attention to the places they passed and the people they met. He stored up in his memory all the wonders he experienced.

The Silk Road took them, after four years of dangerous and difficult traveling, to the fabulous court of Kublai Khan. Kublai Khan was delighted to see the Italians and wanted to learn all about life in Europe.

Over the next 17 years, Kublai Khan sent Marco Polo on special missions to many different parts of Asia. While his uncle and father remained at the Mongol court, Marco traveled widely. Among the places he visited are India, Burma (**bur**•muh), Malaya (muh•**lay**•uh), Sri Lanka (sree **lahng**•kuh), Sumatra (su•**mah**•truh), Java (**jah**•vuh), and Tibet. These travels are the basis of his famous book.

After 17 years at Kublai Khan's court, the Polos wanted to return home. Kublai Khan at first did not want to let the

Did You Know?

Kublai Khan lived from 1215 to 1294. He was the grandson of Genghis Khan, the Mongolian warrior who conquered much of Asia. Kublai inherited the empire from his grandfather. While he could be cruel to his enemies, he promoted literature and art in China. He was eager to learn about European culture and that is why he welcomed the Polos.

Italians leave. He finally allowed them to go, if they would perform one final mission. He asked them to escort a Mongol princess to her wedding in Persia. The Polos sailed across the Indian Ocean to the Persian port of Hormuz. After saying good-bye to the princess, they traveled by land to the Mediterranean coast and sailed home to Venice. They had been away for 24 years.

Marco Polo

Several years after their return, Venice was at war with another Italian city. Marco Polo became a soldier and was captured. He shared a cell with a well-known writer named Rustichello (roo•stee•**kel**•loh). To pass the time, Marco Polo told his cellmate all about his travels in Asia. Rustichello realized that Marco Polo's stories would make a terrific book and began to write them down. By the time they were released from prison, the book was finished. Rustichello was right. *The Travels of Marco Polo* became one of the most popular books of the Middle Ages as soon as it was published in 1299.

It's no mystery why Marco Polo's book was such a sensation. He described strange animals, like the crocodile. He discussed customs unheard of in Europe, such as a post office, paper money, and heating with coal. He told about incredible, gold-covered temples; rubies as large as a man's hand; printed books; and colorful fireworks that used a strange black powder—gunpowder!

Fact or Fiction?

There are still many historians who question whether Marco Polo ever made it to China. Polo's own accounts of his adventures provide most of the documentation that we have. Chinese sources of the period talk about foreigners at the court of Kublai Khan, but there is no mention of Marco Polo or any other Italians.

In his book, Polo talks about amazing things that he saw during his travels. But the things that he doesn't mention are what make historians question the accuracy of his accounts. Polo never mentions the Great Wall of China, Chinese tea-drinking ceremonies, or the custom of binding young girls' feet. Travelers that have tried to retrace his steps have been unable to go further east than Constantinople.

So how was Marco Polo able to make maps and record the geography of the places he claimed to have visited? Some believe that he gathered the information from other traders and copied details from Persian and Arabic guidebooks that his family had collected during their travels.

In Polo's defense, many other historians believe that Polo was very loyal to Kublai Khan, the leader of the Mongols. Polo's works were probably written to show the glory of the Mongol Empire. Polo also did not learn the Chinese language. He was not able to read the classics that shaped the culture.

So what do you think? Sometimes we have to gather information from many sources and form our own opinions about what might have happened in history. If you want to know more about Marco Polo, go to the library. Do some research and decide for yourself.

All across Europe, readers were thrilled by Marco Polo's descriptions of the wide world. Some of his tales were so outlandish that people thought he made them up. While there is some exaggeration in his book, historians have found much of what Marco Polo wrote to be accurate. In fact, he claimed on his deathbed, "I have not told half of what I saw!"

The book helped bring about an important change in the feelings of Europeans. They began to wonder about life beyond the continent's borders. They began to want to explore other places. Some brave explorers would even decide to follow in the footsteps of Marco Polo.

An Arab Adventurer

In A.D. 632, a local religious and community leader died in Arabia. In just a few years, he would become one of the most famous and important people in the history of the world. Do you know his name?

The man was the prophet Muhammad (mu•hah•muhd). He was the founder of the religion of Islam. Muhammad dreamed of uniting all the Arab peoples of the Mediterranean and Middle East. In less than 200 years, Muhammad's dream had come true. Islamic civilization expanded to Africa, Asia, Europe, and other parts of the world.

Muslims, believers of the Islam religion, in Arabia and the Mediterranean became curious about how Muslims lived in other parts of the world. This desire to learn about other Muslims, as well as non-Muslims, led many Arabs to become explorers. Arab explorers crossed the awesome Sahara (suh•hair•uh) Desert on camels and journeyed to India on horseback. Most feared the world's oceans, calling them the *Seas of Darkness*. But with time, they began to overcome their fears and became good sailors as well.

In 1325, the greatest of all Arab explorers discovered the excitement of traveling. In that year, a man named Ibn Battuta (**ib**•uhn buh•**too**•tuh) traveled to Mecca (**mek**•uh), the capital of Islam. He found travel so interesting that he decided to see some more of the world—a whole lot more! In his long life, Ibn Battuta traveled about 75,000 miles (120,000 kilometers), enough miles to take him around the world three times!

The dhow was used as transportation in the age of Battuta.

Ibn Battuta was born in Tangier, Morocco (tan•jeer muh•rok•oh), on the northwestern coast of Africa in 1302. His name in Arabic means "the duckling's son!" After going on his **pilgrimage** to Mecca, Ibn Battuta decided to take an ocean voyage. In an Arab ship called a *dhow* (dow), he sailed down the east coast of Africa as far as the modern country of Tanzania (tan•zuh•nee•uh). During his voyage, Ibn Battuta kept detailed notes and records of the people he met and the places he visited. He continued this habit for the rest of his life.

After he returned and spent some time in Mecca, the traveling bug bit Ibn Battuta again. He headed for India by way of Turkey. He made a detour to the north to visit the ruler of a great Muslim empire in what are today Russia, Ukraine (yoo•**krayn**), and the regions around the Caspian (**kas**•pee•uhn) Sea. This empire is known as the *Golden Horde*. Then his explorations took him along the Silk Road. He traveled by caravan through the modern countries of Iran and Afghanistan. Ibn Battuta was following the road traveled only 50 years earlier by Marco Polo and his family.

Ibn Battuta finally made it to India. He stayed several years and became a judge and then the ambassador to China. Now he could explore this country.

However, it took the great traveler several years to make it to China. Shipwrecks, pirate and bandit attacks, wars, and other misfortunes kept him from taking up his post. During this part of his life, Ibn Battuta explored much of India, Sri Lanka, and Sumatra.

After spending time in China, Ibn Battuta wanted to explore more places: Spain and the Kingdom of Mali and its capital city, Timbuktu (tim•buk•**too**).

After exploring Spain, Ibn Battuta set off for Mali (**mah**•lee). Mali was on the other side of the fearsome Sahara Desert, the world's largest desert. The journey was so terrifying that few ever attempted it. If you look at a map of Africa, you'll see how huge and forbidding this hot, dry, empty desert is.

Traveling in a camel caravan, Ibn Battuta battled intense heat, nighttime cold, dangerous blowing sands, and **marauding** bandits. At the few towns and oases, or desert spots with water and trees, the caravan picked up supplies for the next leg of the journey.

Successfully reaching Timbuktu, Ibn Battuta spent about a year in Mali. He also was able to explore the great river that ran through much of western Africa, the Niger (**neye**•juhr). It was so difficult to reach the banks of the Niger that no one explored it for 400 more years after Ibn Battuta saw it!

When Ibn Battuta finally returned to Morocco, he stayed. Like Marco Polo before him, he told the story of his travels to a writer. The book they wrote, called *Rihlah* (**ree**•lah), or Travels, is a very valuable source of information about his time and the world of Islam he explored. Throughout his life, his motto was "Never follow the same road twice." When he died at the age of about 65, he was famous throughout the Muslim world as its greatest traveler and explorer.

The Travels of Ibn Battuta

Contributions of Asian Explorers

Asian explorers made use of important inventions and special knowledge. One invention was the quadrant. The quadrant was an instrument to determine a ship's **latitude**. Using lines drawn on the quadrant, navigators could use stars and planets to find their location north and south. Asians were also excellent mapmakers, combining older maps by Greeks and other civilizations with their own observations.

In addition to these contributions, Asian explorers brought an important Chinese invention to the West—the compass. This magnetized needle pointed out directions to travelers, especially important in crossing wide, empty spaces like deserts and oceans.

key (top)	
Chang Ch'ien	—
Hsuan-tsang	—

key (bottom)	
Marco Polo	—
Ibn Battuta	—

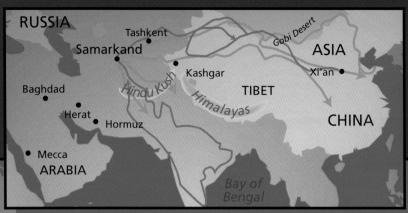

Chapter 3

The Search for El Dorado in South America and Mexico

I n the century following the travels of Ibn Battuta, leadership in world exploration shifted to Europe. Portuguese sailors, under their famous leader Prince Henry, explored the west coast of Africa. They dreamed of finding a sea route to the riches of India and China, one that would be shorter and safer than the land route used by Marco Polo. Many of the explorers used Ptolemy's map. They had no idea that two huge continents sat on the other side of the Atlantic.

It wouldn't be long before they found out, though. King Ferdinand and Queen Isabella of Spain knew that finding a faster route to China and India would make Spain rich. In

1492, they sent an Italian captain on a voyage that would change the way people thought about their world. His name was Christopher Columbus. If you look at Ptolemy's map, you may not be surprised that Columbus believed that the land he explored was Japan, not North and Central America. Even though he was mistaken, his voyage to the New World began a great age of exploration.

Other explorers who lived after Columbus came to understand that America, not Japan, was the land that lay on the other side of the Atlantic Ocean. This new, unexplored land fired their imaginations with new dreams.

Search for the Golden Man

One of these powerful new dreams was known as *El Dorado* (el duh•rah•doh), Spanish for "the golden man." At the beginning of the 1500s, Spanish explorers began to hear legends and tales about an unbelievably rich kingdom, somewhere in the New World. The ruler of this fabulous kingdom was the Golden Man. He was so wealthy that each morning his servants covered him with a sticky substance. Then they sprinkled him with gold dust, so he would resemble the sun! The Golden Man would then bathe in a holy lake, and his people would throw gold objects into the lake after him!

This legend drove some Spanish explorers almost crazy with greed. Where could they find this Golden Man? How could they get their hands on this gold-filled lake and all the other treasures of such a kingdom? As the legend of El Dorado was passed from person to person, it grew. In no time, the Golden Man had become a golden city, or even a golden kingdom. Buildings were made of solid gold, and the streets were paved, not with rocks, but with diamonds!

Although it might sound a little crazy to us today, the legend of El Dorado did have a bit of truth in it. The Indian civilizations of the New World were rich in gold and silver. Both the Aztecs (**az**•teks) in modern-day Mexico and the Incas (**ing**•kuhz) of South America were wealthy. Historians believe that a ceremony similar in some ways to the Golden Man legend actually took place at a lake near Bogotá, Colombia (boh•guh•**tah** kuh•**lum**•bee•uh).

In the early 1500s, these peoples became the targets of Spanish explorers. The Spanish adventurers who sailed to the New World in search of gold and power were known as *conquistadors* (kong•**kee**•stuh•dorz). This word comes from the Spanish word for "conquerors." In addition to conquering great civilizations, these conquistadors also explored great areas of unknown territory in North, Central, and South America. They came in search of El Dorado, and in the process, they destroyed empires.

Hernan Cortés Discovers the Aztec Empire

By 1519, the Spanish had already established colonies on the island of Cuba and in Panama. Rumors of unbelievably rich cities on the mainland reached these colonies. Hernan Cortés (air•**nahn** kor•**tez**) had heard stories of a rich empire in Mexico. He was about to become one of the first Spanish conquistadors. Promises of gold and silver made it easy for Cortés to find 600 adventurers to join his exploration party. He and his troops landed on the Mexican shore and began their march toward the capital city of the Aztec empire, Tenochtitlán (teh•nawch•tee•**tlahn**).

Who were the Aztecs? They were a Native American people who founded their city and empire in the early 1300s. Their culture was advanced in many ways. They had their own system of writing, and knew much about agriculture, science, and art. Their capital city of Tenochtitlán was built in the middle of a lake, with canals instead of streets. One Spaniard said the city looked like "an enchanted vision."

The Aztec religion, however, was a cruel one. They believed that the sun god died each night and would only be reborn the next day if he were given a live human. Consequently, the Aztecs made human sacrifices to the sun god daily. This disturbed the Spanish greatly, and they felt justified in conquering the empire.

When Cortés and his men arrived at Tenochtitlán, the Aztec king, Montezuma (mon•teh•**zoo**•mah), believed they were gods, whose coming had been **foretold**.

Depiction of Cortés and Montezuma

Who else but gods, he thought, could have powerful weapons like cannons and muskets and ride strange animals like horses? The Aztecs had never seen any of these things! Montezuma welcomed the Spaniards and offered them gifts. He hoped his generosity would convince them to leave the Aztecs alone, but he was wrong.

The gifts Montezuma gave to Cortés and his men only made the Spaniards want more. Cortés took the Aztec king prisoner and held him for **ransom**. Although the Aztecs paid the Spanish a huge amount of gold, Cortés did not release Montezuma. Fighting broke out, and many Aztecs and Spaniards were killed. Montezuma was killed by his own people, who had become angry at his rule. Cortés and his troops surrounded the Aztecs. Many starved, but even more deadly was the outbreak of a disease called *smallpox*. The Spanish had brought it to Mexico, and the Indians could not fight off the illness.

Tenochtitlán finally fell, and the Spanish emptied the vast Aztec **treasuries**. Then Cortés destroyed the city. On its ruins, the Spanish built the town now called *Mexico City*. Only a few years after the arrival of the conquistadors, the mighty Aztec empire was no more.

Pizarro Conquers the Incas

Cortés was the first conquistador, but others soon followed the dream of El Dorado. As they searched for the legend, the Spanish visited large areas of North and South America. They were the first Europeans to explore the New World. Another great Indian civilization ruled in much of the region of the Andes Mountains of South America. These were the Incas. Like the Aztecs in Mexico, they would soon suffer dreadfully because of the dream of El Dorado. To them, it became a nightmare.

The Inca Empire in modern-day Ecuador (ek•wuh•dor) and Peru had expanded greatly during the fourteenth and fifteenth centuries. It probably had six to eight million inhabitants, governed by a ruler known as the *Inca*. The Inca people were great engineers and builders. Their cities were beautiful and wealthy.

About 10 years after Cortés destroyed the Aztecs, another Spaniard named Francisco Pizarro (frahn•sees•koh pee•zar•oh) landed in what is today Peru. He too had heard rumors of an incredibly rich kingdom, where gold was as cheap and as common as iron. With his small force, Pizarro crossed the Andes. This region is known for its treacherous mountain ledges covered with ice and snow. Pizarro and his men were the first Europeans to see the unusual animals of the Andes, like the **alpaca**, the **vicuna**, and the awesome Andean **condor**, with a wingspan of 10 feet (3 meters) or more.

However, like other conquistadors, Pizarro and his men were not interested in unusual wildlife. They attacked Cuzco (**koo**•skoh), the capital city of the Incas. The Incas, weakened by civil war, could not defend themselves from the horses, guns, swords, and armor of the Spanish. Pizarro led his men from city to city, looting gold and silver as they went, and eventually killing the king. As in Mexico, the Inca Empire vanished soon after the arrival of the European invaders. The Spaniards quarreled over how to rule the Incas, and Pizarro was murdered by rivals in 1541.

Incan ruins

Francisco de Orellana Meets the Amazon

Francisco Pizarro had a brother who was also a conquistador. Gonzalo (gon•zah•loh) Pizarro looked for El Dorado across the Andes from Peru. He wanted to explore the jungle regions surrounding a river called the *Napo* (nah•poh). The Spaniards hoped they might find even more gold.

However, travel was extremely difficult through the thick jungle. In many ways, it was even harder than the mountains. Strange creatures shrieked at the men from the treetops, while huge snakes slithered through the underbrush. Flesh-eating **piranhas** patrolled the rivers. The heat and humidity were intense, and it rained for two months straight! Food was very scarce.

Gonzalo Pizarro and most of his desperate men decided to try to return home. But Francisco de Orellana (frahn•sees•koh day oh•ray•lyah•nah), one of the crew, pressed on with about 50 others. As they floated slowly downstream, the river widened with every mile. The Indians they met, although some were friendly, attacked the Spaniards often. Can you guess the name of the great river Orellana was exploring? Here's the story of how it got its name.

Naming a Great River

One of the tribes that attacked the Spanish seemed to be composed of only women. These tall women warriors were excellent fighters. A Spaniard wrote, "With their bows and arrows in their hands, they do as much fighting as ten Indian men." Historians now believe that the warriors the Spanish saw were probably men with long hair. However, they reminded the Spanish of the *Amazon women,* fierce women warriors from ancient Greek legends. The explorers named the river they traveled the *Amazon* after the legendary warriors.

The Amazon River winds through South America.

31

The Amazon

The Amazon River is almost 4,000 miles long, second in length only to the Nile River in Africa. It follows on a line parallel to and a little south of the equator. Seven miles across at its widest, it is fed by more than 1,000 **tributaries**. The river dumps 3.5 million gallons of water into the Atlantic every minute.

After their long journey down the Amazon, the Spaniards came to a place where the river was so wide they could not see banks on either side! Because of this, they knew they must be near the river's mouth. Sure enough, they soon reached the Atlantic Ocean, in what is today northern Brazil. They had explored the world's second-longest river, trailing only Africa's Nile. From source to mouth, the Spanish had traveled about 4,000 miles (6,440 kilometers) on the Amazon and the smaller rivers that feed it. This region is so difficult to travel through that some of it still remains unexplored today! Even with modern equipment, very few explorers have been able to follow Orellana! Today, the Amazon **Basin** is the world's largest unexplored region.

Did you Know...

. . . how the continents of the Western Hemisphere came to be known as the Americas? In 1501, an Italian sailor named Amerigo Vespucci, sailing for Spain, explored the northeastern coast of South America. In 1507, his letters were published. The publisher provided a map, with the New World labeled "America," after the Italian who helped explore it. The name has stuck ever since!

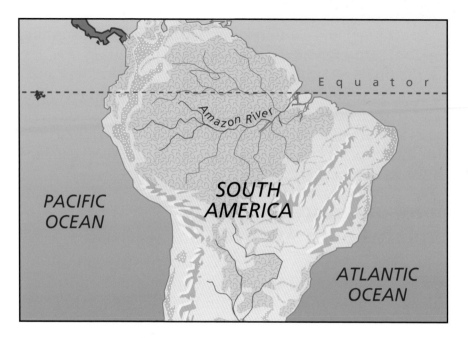

La Condamine Studies the Equator

As the years passed, explorers from countries other than Spain or Portugal accepted the challenge of South America. In 1735, a French scientist named Charles-Marie de La Condamine (sharl-mar•ee du lah con•dah•**meen**) was sent on a mission by the king of France. His task was to measure the curve of the earth's surface along the equator. The equator is an imaginary line drawn horizontally around the middle of the earth.

Look at a map of the world and you'll see right away how difficult La Condamine's task was. The equator runs right through some of the thickest parts of the Amazon rain forest and jungle. It's impossible to even walk anywhere, much less use equipment to measure from one point to another!

As it turned out, La Condamine spent seven years in the Amazon. Although he did not finish his measuring task, he was the first to scientifically explore the Amazon River and the jungles around it. La Condamine kept detailed records about river depth and width and about all the strange plants and animals he saw. He was especially **intrigued** with rubber plants and electric eels, which are fish that can deliver a strong electric shock.

Humboldt and Bonpland Explore South America

More than 50 years after La Condamine studied the Amazon, another great European explorer and scientist added even more to our understanding of the land and nature of South America. Alexander von Humboldt (ah•lik•**sahn**•duhr von **hum**•bohlt) was a well-known German scientist whose training included engineering, foreign languages, mining, and many other areas. In 1799, he decided to set off for South America. His mother had died and had left him enough money to finance the expedition. Humboldt chose a French scientist named Aimé Bonpland (eh•**may** bon•**plahn**) to accompany him on the trip. They were to spend the next five years in the deepest jungles and highest mountain ranges of South America.

Humboldt and Bonpland first explored the Orinoco (or•uh•**noh**•koh) River, which empties into the Atlantic in present-day Venezuela. One of the discoveries they made was that the Orinoco and the Amazon were linked by a series of smaller rivers. Humboldt and Bonpland focused especially on the plant and animal life of the region and collected thousands of samples. Most of the plants and many of the animals were unknown anywhere else. While in the region, Humboldt and Bonpland performed many experiments. Humboldt swallowed *curare* (ku•**rah**•ree), a deadly poison used by local Indians to tip their arrows and spears. Humboldt believed that it was dangerous only when it entered the blood through a break in the skin. He turned out to be right, but would you have swallowed it like he did to prove your point? Another experiment Humboldt performed was to have Bonpland hold one end of an electric eel while he held the other! What do you think happened? The result was shocking!

Humboldt also climbed mountains, including volcanoes. He scaled a mountain called *Chimborazo* (cheem•boh•**rah**•zoh), near Quito (**kee**•toh), Ecuador, reaching a height of 19,280 feet (5,877 meters). It remained the world mountaineering record for 30 years, and Humboldt did it without oxygen, ropes, or special mountaineering equipment! When he finally returned to Europe, Humboldt was a hero. He was even called the *Napoleon of science,* after the great French emperor.

Did You Know?

Alexander von Humboldt discovered many plants and animals during his expedition to South America. Some of them were named after him. One of these was a type of monkey that was later in danger of extinction. He would be pleased to know that the species survived and is no longer in danger.

Humboldt's woolly monkey

Exploring South America and Mexico

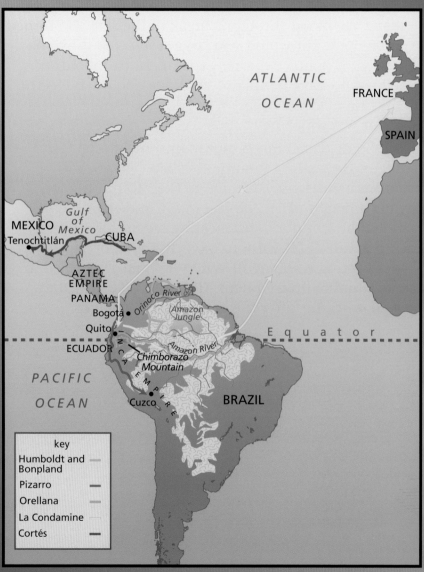

ATLANTIC OCEAN

FRANCE

SPAIN

Gulf of Mexico

MEXICO
Tenochtitlán

CUBA

AZTEC EMPIRE

PANAMA

Bogotá

Orinoco River

Amazon Jungle

Quito

Equator

ECUADOR

INCA EMPIRE

Chimborazo Mountain

Amazon River

Cuzco

BRAZIL

PACIFIC OCEAN

key

Humboldt and Bonpland

Pizarro

Orellana

La Condamine

Cortés

Chapter 4

Following the Legend to North America

The legend of El Dorado was so powerful that other explorers looked for it in what is now the United States of America. By this time, there were many different tales of great wealth to be found in the New World. The riches in the New World appeared to be never-ending, and the Europeans were determined to find them.

Juan Ponce de León and the Fountain of Youth

One legend led another Spanish explorer to Florida. His name was Juan Ponce de León (wahn **pahn**•suh day **lee**•ohn). Do you know what he was looking for?

Ponce de León imagined a fantastic fountain of youth.

His dream might seem even more far-fetched than a city made of gold. Ponce de León was on the trail of a fountain that cured all diseases and kept people who drank from it young and healthy forever. According to the myth, anyone who drank from the fountain would have **eternal** youth. De León was so excited about the legend that he organized his own expedition to find the fountain. If they were successful, he would gain great fame and wealth.

Ponce de León and his crew left the port of San Germán, Puerto Rico (sahn her•**mahn pwair**•toh **ree**•koh), with three ships in March of 1513. They sailed northwest, stopping at San Salvador (san **sal**•vuh•dor) for a few days. From there, they continued sailing northwest until they sighted land on April 2, which was the week before Easter. They landed on the mainland near the site of the modern-day city of St. Augustine (saynt **aw**•guh•steen), Florida.

Like so many explorers, Ponce de León was a little confused. He did not realize that he had landed on a continent. He thought he had landed on the island of Bimini (**bim**•uh•nee), home of the legendary Fountain of Youth. He named the new land Florida, perhaps because of the beautiful flowers he found there—*Florida* means "flowery" in Spanish—or in honor of the Easter holiday, which is *la pascua florida* (lah **pahs**•kwah flo•**ree**•dah) in Spanish. The next day, he took possession of the land in the name of the king of Spain.

A few days later, Ponce de León and his group sailed south. There they made an important discovery. As they sailed, a very heavy current called the *Gulf Stream* slowed them down. The discovery opened a new route for travel from Spain to North America.

While Ponce de León never found the Fountain of Youth, he did find plenty of swamps and mosquitoes. He is credited with being the first European to see and explore Florida. The place where he first landed became the settlement of St. Augustine, the oldest city in the United States.

Hernando de Soto

Remember Francisco Pizarro and the conquest of the Incas? A man named Hernando de Soto (er•**nahn**•doh di **soh**•toh) participated in the Inca expedition. It made him a very rich man. When he returned to Spain in 1536, he was given an important position as governor of Cuba. The position gave de Soto the right to conquer and colonize the territory north of Cuba on the mainland of North America. It would later become known as Florida.

De Soto and six hundred men sailed from Cuba in 1539. They landed near Tampa Bay in Florida. By the fall of that year, they reached the Indian village of Apalachee (ap•uh•**lach**•ee), near what is now Tallahassee. De Soto and his troops spent the winter there, despite the hostile Native American tribes in the area.

When spring came, they left in search of their treasure. De Soto and his troops had heard about a place called *Cofitachequi*. Legends said that it was ruled by a powerful and wealthy queen. Traveling northward into what is now Georgia in the spring of 1540, de Soto soon reached the Indian village. The Cofitachequi leader was a woman named Cutifachiqui. The villagers welcomed de Soto and his men with gifts of food and worthless freshwater pearls. However, de Soto was not disappointed. He was convinced that this was a sign of great treasures nearby.

The expedition continued. Every time the explorers came to a village, they demanded to know where the gold was kept. When the people of the tribes protested that they had no gold, de Soto had them tortured. He and his men pressed on to the north, hoping to find their treasure. Their journey of exploration took them as far north as what are now Tennessee, North Carolina, and the foothills of the Great Smoky Mountains. The party turned west and wandered through Alabama and Mississippi.

On May 21, 1541, de Soto's band reached the banks of a great river flowing from north to south. The Native Americans called it *Father of the Water*. We know it as the Mississippi. De Soto's men were the first Europeans to see America's grandest river. The Spaniards crossed the river and explored Louisiana and Arkansas, battling Native Americans and disease the whole way. De Soto himself caught a fever and died in 1542. His men buried his body in the Father of the Water and continued on. They reached Spanish settlements in Mexico later that year.

Francisco Coronado

Meanwhile, further west, another conquistador named Francisco Coronado (frahn•sees•koh kor•uh•nah•doh) went looking for the legendary Seven Cities of Cíbola (see•buh•luh). He had heard tales that these magnificent cities had walls built of gold and turquoise. They were thought to be somewhere north of Mexico.

According to a guide named Friar Marcos (fry•uhr mar•kohs), the Native Americans of Cíbola made everything out of gold. The cities were larger and more wonderful than those of Tenochtitlán. He told wonderful stories of buildings ten stories high and temples covered with turquoise. Marcos offered to lead an expedition to the cities. It was exactly what Coronado had been hoping for.

The party left Mexico in 1540. They traveled for four months and 1,500 miles (2,414 kilometers) through the desert. The Spanish sighted the first of the Seven Cities of Cíbola on July 4, 1540, in what is now northern New Mexico. What do you think they saw? Instead of a wealthy city, the conquistadors found the adobe huts of the Native American pueblo (pweb•loh), or village. They quickly sent patrols out to look for the other six cities. All of them were the same. The Seven Cities of Cíbola turned out to be as phony as El Dorado!

A pueblo structure in New Mexico

However, Coronado and his men did make some very interesting discoveries. They marveled at the immense herds of "large shaggy cattle" they saw roaming the plains. Can you guess what they were? The Spaniards were seeing bison, or buffalo, by the millions. One of Coronado's officers became the first European to stand at the edge of an incredible natural wonder. In what is now Arizona, Lopez de Cardenas (**loh**•pes day **kar**•day•nahs) gazed out over the Grand Canyon.

Exploring North America

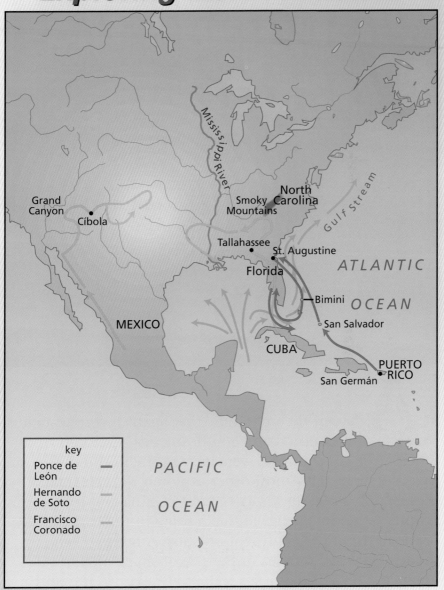

Grand Canyon

Cíbola

Mississippi River

Smoky Mountains

North Carolina

Tallahassee

Florida

St. Augustine

Gulf Stream

ATLANTIC

OCEAN

Bimini

San Salvador

MEXICO

CUBA

PUERTO RICO

San Germán

PACIFIC

OCEAN

key

Ponce de León —

Hernando de Soto —

Francisco Coronado —

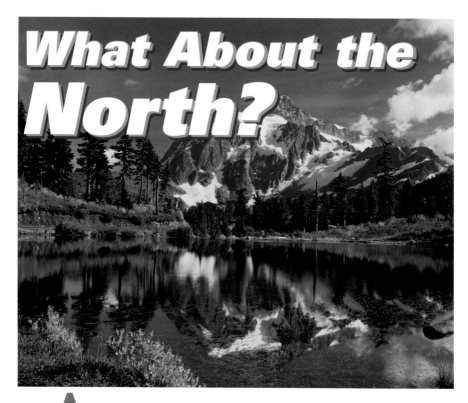

Chapter 5

What About the North?

At about the same time that Spanish conquistadors were exploring Central and South America, explorers from other European countries were busy in the northern part of North America. Like most other explorers of their time, they were looking for a way to sail to China and India. People of the time believed that a route to the East existed to the north of the continent of North America. Even though they had no idea of the size or shape of North America, they felt that a sea route must exist to the north.

This unknown route was called the *Northwest Passage*. Many brave sailors lost their lives exploring the freezing oceans around the North Pole. Beginning in the late 1500s, adventurers began to explore the wilderness of today's Canada and the northern United States. In the end, they did not find gold or silver, and the Northwest Passage remained uncharted for centuries. But they did find something almost as valuable as gold. The lumber in the dense forests of North America was a valuable **commodity**. The explorers also created an important trading network, founded settlements that grew into great cities, and spread the ideas and values of their countries.

Jacques Cartier Searches for the Northwest Passage

One country that was very intent on finding the Northwest Passage was France. Their explorers claimed many new areas of the New World for France. Today, their presence can still be seen throughout northern North America.

The first step in the building of New France was taken by Jacques Cartier (zhahk kar•**tyay**). In 1534, he sailed to the northeast coast of Canada. He explored Newfoundland (**noo**•fuhn•luhnd), Prince Edward Island, and Labrador (**lab**•ruh•dor). Cartier also sighted a large, wide opening in the forest, which he thought was a bay. He returned to France as winter approached, with no news to report about a Northwest Passage.

The next year he returned to Canada and the bay he had seen earlier. This time, Native Americans told him it was not a bay, but in fact, a great river. They also told Cartier the river led to the fabulously wealthy kingdom of Saguenay (sag•uh•nay). Here they said Cartier would find riches as great as those of the Aztecs and Incas. Cartier was thrilled. He envisioned the kingdom to be in China at the end of the Northwest Passage. Excitedly, he followed the river, the St. Lawrence, which runs 800 miles (1,287 kilometers) from Lake Ontario to the Atlantic Ocean.

To his great disappointment, Cartier found no rich kingdoms, only small Native American villages. One of these villages was located on a mountain. Cartier named the mountain *Mount Royal*, in honor of the French king. Does its name sound familiar? This place later grew into the great Canadian city of Montreal.

The British Give It a Go!

An English expedition to find the Northwest Passage began in 1576. Under the command of Martin Frobisher (**froh**•bi•shuhr), three ships set sail from London. When they reached the coast of Greenland, they were blocked by ice. Finally, after a disastrous journey, one ship was able to continue. Soon Frobisher reached what he believed to be the approach to the Northwest Passage.

He was so excited that he named the area *Frobisher's Strait*. He had no idea that it was only an inlet for Baffin (**baf**•in) Island and led nowhere. While he was exploring the inlet, Frobisher met the Inuit Native Americans. He thought their features looked Asian, and he became convinced that he had made it to the Northwest Passage.

Frobisher found something that caught his interest on Baffin Island. The island was full of sparkling stones.

Frobisher believed that what he was seeing was gold—and it was everywhere! He gathered as much of the rock as he could and rushed back to England. Experts declared that it was indeed gold.

He had set out to find the Northwest Passage, but now Frobisher believed he had discovered something even more valuable. He made two more journeys to Baffin Island. Each time he brought back as much of the rock as he could. When he finally returned from his third voyage, he was told that the rocks he had collected were worthless. They had been identified as *iron pyrite,* also known as *fool's gold.* As you may have guessed, Frobisher returned to England in disgrace.

Getting Around

Do you know which way of traveling was most popular for the early explorers of the Great Lakes? Here's a clue: It's a special kind of boat, first made by the Native Americans who lived in the region. It's the canoe. This light, nimble boat comes in all shapes and sizes, but most are long and narrow. All canoes are paddled, and they are light enough to be carried around rapids and waterfalls.

When Martin Frobisher first came upon Baffin Island, the Inuits skimmed across the water in one-person canoes called kayaks. The kayaks were made from wooden frames covered with sealskins. From a distance, the British thought the kayaks were seals or large fish.

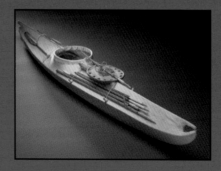

Champlain Goes Up the St. Lawrence to the Great Lakes

The next great French explorer was Samuel de Champlain (**sam**•yoo•uhl duh sham•**playn**). Champlain is known as the explorer of the Great Lakes. He was a very unusual European explorer. Unlike most other Europeans, he trusted and admired many of the Native Americans he met on his explorations. He was most friendly with the Huron (**hyur**•on) and Algonquin (al•**gong**•kwin) Native Americans.

Champlain traveled up the St. Lawrence River for the first time in 1604. He returned to France and spread the news about the region around the St. Lawrence. He sailed for New France the next year and remained for three long, hard winters. During the first winter, half of his men died of scurvy, a disease caused by a lack of vitamin C. On his third journey to New France, he founded a colony. You've probably heard of it—Quebec (kwi•**bek**), today one of Canada's great cities.

Champlain also had another talent that proved extremely useful. He was a cartographer (kar•**tog**•ruh•fuhr), or professional mapmaker. The maps he made of the Great Lakes region were important steps to understanding the New World. They gave other explorers a much better idea of what the Great Lakes looked like. By the time he died in 1635, Champlain had strengthened France's presence in North America. He had seen his colony of Quebec grow into a small town, and he had discovered several important lakes and rivers. Samuel de Champlain is known as the Father of New France.

Crossing the Atlantic

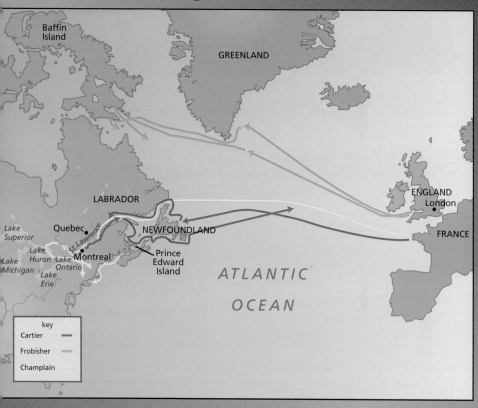

Chapter 6

Moving Westward

Exploring the Western Frontier

I n the last chapter, you read about the hardy adventurers who explored the eastern part of North America. In the West, however, things were different. High mountain ranges made land travel difficult. The rivers flowed into the Pacific Ocean, so boat travel was limited. Native American tribes were less familiar. Exploring grew more dangerous as the distances from home increased. But it was not in the explorers' nature to look for the easy way. They were looking for excitement, adventure, and gold. And that is exactly what they found in the West.

Robert de La Salle

In the years following the settlement of New France, explorers from both France and Britain slowly pushed the **frontier** westward. A frontier is the borderline between known and unknown regions. One of the best known of these explorers is Robert de La Salle (roh•**bair** duh lah **sal**), a Frenchman.

In 1678, King Louis XIV sent La Salle to the New World. Explorers had heard stories and legends from the Native Americans about a great sea to the west of North America. The French decided that this western sea must be the Pacific and that it was possible to reach it by a land route. La Salle's mission was to investigate these legends and try to follow the rivers of North America to the western sea. He was also ordered to build a series of forts to help the French expand their fur-trading empire toward the West.

La Salle was a man who wanted not only to explore new regions but to receive all the glory for his discoveries. His desire for fame made him many enemies and sometimes made his plans hard to carry out. It took him several years to get ready for his journey.

In 1679, he assembled his party just upstream of a huge waterfall the Native Americans called *Niagara* (neye•**ag**•ruh). The waterfall lies between Lake Ontario and Lake Erie. If you have ever been to Niagara Falls, you know what an impressive sight it must have been for La Salle and his men.

La Salle's route took him through Lake Huron and Lake Michigan to the mouth of the Illinois River. The Illinois River empties into the Mississippi. On the banks of the Illinois, La Salle built a fort. He called it *Fort Heartbreak,* for all the miseries the journey had caused. From Fort Heartbreak, he and his party traveled on the Illinois to the Mississippi. Near where another mighty river, the Ohio, meets the Mississippi, he built another fort.

On April 6, 1682, after three years of trying, La Salle finally reached the mouth of the Mississippi. Three days later, in a magnificent ceremony, La Salle claimed all the land drained by the great river for France. He named it Louisiana, in honor of his king.

La Salle claimed the Mississippi on behalf of France.

Believe it or not, King Louis was not at all happy about Louisiana! He felt that it would be too hard for France to look after such a huge area—and he was probably right. However, after a while, Louis changed his mind and sent La Salle on another mission to the New World. He was to establish new French colonies in what is now the southern United States. Louis hoped to use the new colonies to attack Spain's wealthy empire in Mexico.

Things did not go well for La Salle this time. Sailing through the Gulf of Mexico, he could not find the mouth of the Mississippi. Lost, he found himself in Matagorda (ma•tuh•gor•duh) Bay, in southern Texas. The members of his party grew increasingly worried. Finally, La Salle decided to march overland back to the Illinois River for help. Some of his angry men **rebelled** and killed La Salle.

A War and a Sale Open Up the West for Exploration

The western frontier presented many challenges to explorers. But there were other things going on in the New World, too. The successful ending of the Revolutionary War in 1783 created a new country in North America, the United States. The young country was made up of 13 states along the eastern coast of the continent. However, the American people soon began moving westward in search of new lands. New states and territories joined the union. Then, in 1803, something happened that would change the world forever.

Do you remember what the French explorer Robert de La Salle did when he stood at the mouth of the Mississippi

River in 1682? He claimed all the land that drained into the great river for France. As the 1800s began, it became clear that whichever country controlled the Mississippi River and the trade of its busy port of New Orleans would have a great advantage. But Napoleon, the ruler of France, needed money to fight wars in Europe. He offered to sell the huge Louisiana Territory to the United States.

President Thomas Jefferson agreed to the sale, but he worried that the territory was just too gigantic for the United States to control. It would more than double the size of the country overnight! Jefferson decided the offer was too good to pass up, and Louisiana became part of the United States. The country now stretched from the Atlantic Ocean to the Rocky Mountains.

Lewis and Clark

But what was the new territory like? Who lived there? Did it contain valuable natural resources? What plants grew there? What animals roamed the region? To answer these questions, Jefferson, in 1804, sent Meriwether Lewis and William Clark on a journey through the new lands. This journey is known as the *Lewis and Clark Expedition*. An expedition is a long trip with a specific goal. For Lewis and Clark, the goal was to explore the newly purchased Louisiana Territory.

The expedition left from St. Louis, which at that time was a small riverside town near the place where the Mississippi and Missouri Rivers meet. Lewis and Clark's two-year journey of discovery took them all the way to the Pacific Ocean.

The first part of Lewis and Clark's journey was through well-traveled country up the Missouri River. When they met Native American tribes along the way, they informed them that their territory was now part of the United States. As they traveled deeper into what would later be North Dakota, they encountered lands and tribes that no American had ever visited before. They knew they would need guides and interpreters for the territories that lay ahead.

Lewis and Clark also had another problem. It would not be long before the men would have to abandon their boats and travel over land, because the Rocky Mountains lay ahead. They would need to trade their boats for pack-horses from a Native American tribe called the *Shoshone* (shoh•**shoh**•nee), who were said to breed excellent horses.

As luck would have it, the interpreter they hired had a wife who was Shoshone. Her name was Sacagawea (sak•uh•juh•**wee**•uh), which means "Bird Woman." She had been born Shoshone but had been captured by the Hidatsa (hee•**daht**•sah) tribe when she was young. There, she was renamed Sacagawea and forced to work in the fields by her captors.

Lewis and Clark insisted on taking Sacagawea on the journey. They knew she would be valuable in negotiations for horses from the Shoshone. Soon, Sacagawea proved that she could do much more than that. A few weeks after she joined the group, a strong wind tipped the lead boat on its side, spilling the contents into the Missouri River. While the passengers in the boat raced to shore, Sacagawea calmly retrieved the floating bundles. They contained the expedition's surveying instruments, maps, medicine, and other essential supplies. Had she not saved them, the expedition would have been forced to turn back.

When Lewis and Clark's expedition reached the Shoshone tribe, the Native Americans seemed less than friendly. But Sacagawea recognized members of the tribe, and later the Shoshone sold Lewis and Clark packhorses and led the travelers partway through the Rocky Mountains.

The Rocky Mountains proved to be one of the most difficult parts of the expedition. The group trudged through knee-deep snow and crossed dangerous mountains in order to reach the Great Divide. Here, the rivers began to flow from east to west—into the Pacific Ocean. If they could find their way to the great Columbia River, they knew they could sail to the sea. With the help of the Nez Percé (nay pair•**say**) Native Americans, they made canoes.

Sacagawea was instrumental in the success of Lewis and Clark.

The group set off down the river in October of 1805, leaving their horses and extra supplies behind with the tribe.

The journey to the Pacific was not an easy one. The many rapids and waterfalls along the way forced the expedition to carry their boats and equipment over land. As they approached the mouth of the Columbia River where it joined the Pacific, there was little celebration. The waters were so rough and the expedition members so seasick that they set up camp several miles from the ocean. They spent the winter there, exploring the coast. They began their journey home in the spring.

When they got back to Washington, D.C., Lewis and Clark were given a hero's welcome. Both of them received large land grants and were given important government posts. During their expedition, Lewis and Clark made maps, crossed mountains, and rafted the rivers. Thanks to their bravery, the United States learned much about the new territory it had acquired.

Mountain Man Jedediah Smith

In the years following the Lewis and Clark Expedition, daring adventurers began to spread out through the West. Because much of their exploration took place in the Rocky Mountains and surrounding areas, they were called *Mountain Men.*

Jedediah Smith was that type of explorer. When Smith was a young boy growing up in Pennsylvania, he read a book about Lewis and Clark. The thrilling adventures of these two explorers excited the young boy's imagination. He promised himself he would one day follow in their footsteps. After finding work with a fur company in

St. Louis, Smith was sent on his first trip to the West between 1822 and 1823. He was among the first large group of trappers to venture into that region.

On his next trip, Smith was put in charge of the expedition. They went to trap in the central Rockies and Columbia River areas. Smith led his 11 men down the White River and through the Badlands of the Dakotas and the Black Hills.

Things were not always easy. While crossing the Badlands, the group nearly died of thirst. In the Black Hills, young Jedediah Smith came face to face with instant death—wilderness style! He was attacked by a grizzly bear, 900 pounds (410 kilograms) of an angry meat eater! Smith lived, but the bear ripped one of his ears almost off his head, along with part of his scalp. Smith had his mates sew him back together. After this attack, Smith began to earn a reputation for toughness few could match.

It turned out that Smith was an excellent trapper. After a while, Smith became the owner of a fur company. He wanted to find new areas for trapping, so he set off in 1826 to explore the West. Even though he found few animals to trap, he did explore great stretches of the American West for the first time. His route took him first to the Great Salt Lake in today's Utah. He headed southwest to the Colorado River, where Arizona and Nevada meet, passing through dry desert country. Then he followed the river to the fertile, green Mojave (moh•hah•vee) Valley. There, he met the Mojave Native Americans.

The Mojave told Smith that just to the west lay a cruel desert, which only they could cross safely. On the other side, however, lay the rich California territory, then controlled by Mexico. With the help of Mojave guides, Smith and his men took 15 days to cross the Mojave Desert. It was so hot that the travelers had to bury themselves in sand to stay cool and avoid the dreadful daytime heat.

Finally, the band emerged on the other side and climbed the San Bernardino (san bur•nuh•**dee**•noh) Mountains. Below them spread the Mexican town of San Gabriel (san **gay**•bree•uhl), which later came to be known as Los Angeles. Because the Mexican rulers of California did not want Americans nosing around, they ordered Smith and his party to leave the way they came.

However, Smith feared crossing the Mojave again, and the band turned north. They found good trapping country along the American River, near present-day Sacramento. However, they missed something even more valuable. In this very place, about 20 years later, gold was found at Sutter's Mill! This discovery sparked the great California Gold Rush of 1849.

Smith and his group tried to cross the Sierra (see•**air**•uh) Mountains. However, the dangerous mountain passes were covered with snow and ice, and they had to turn back. While most of the men stayed behind in California, Smith and two others tried again to cross the fearsome peaks.

They succeeded in crossing the mountains, but soon found themselves in an even more dangerous situation. After the mountains came the Great Basin, a huge desert between the Sierras and the Rockies. The Great Basin had almost no water or food and scorching temperatures. It was 300 miles (480 kilometers) across.

While crossing this desert, one of Smith's friends became too weak to continue. The other two could not carry him.

What would you have done? Smith decided to leave the man under a small tree and try to return in time to save his life. Do you think Jedediah Smith expected to be able to save his friend?

Incredibly, Smith found some water and was able to return to rescue the man. All three finally made it across the Great Basin. When they made it home, the others could not believe their eyes. They had given up hope that Smith and his party would ever return from their journey.

Now what do you think Jedediah Smith did next? Did he decide to take a good long rest and recover from his terrible journey? Not quite. The Mountain Man turned right around and went back across the Mojave Desert! Why? The reason tells you something about the kind of person he was. He wanted to go back for the other members of his group, who had stayed behind in California.

Smith reached his friends, and together they headed north to explore Oregon. There, Native Americans killed all but Smith and one other man. After more adventures, Jedediah Smith died the same way. Members of the Comanche (kuh•**man**•chee), a Native American tribe, killed him while he was exploring the Santa Fe Trail.

Smith probably saw more of the American West than any other explorer of his time. The maps he made and the journal he kept helped other people learn about the West. You can even read his journal today! His notes and letters about water sources, the best routes, and other information aided later settlers who followed in his footsteps.

Exploring the Vast Territories of North America

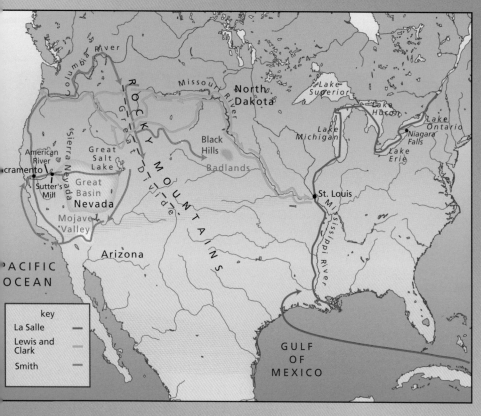

Columbia River

ROCKY MOUNTAINS

Great Divide

Missouri River

North Dakota

Lake Superior

Lake Huron

Lake Michigan

Lake Ontario

Niagara Falls

Lake Erie

Sierra Nevada

Great Salt Lake

Black Hills

Badlands

American River

Sacramento

Sutter's Mill

Great Basin

Nevada

Mojave Valley

Arizona

St. Louis

Mississippi River

PACIFIC OCEAN

key	
La Salle	—
Lewis and Clark	—
Smith	—

GULF OF MEXICO

Chapter 7

The Unknown Continent: Australia

uropeans first discovered Australia in 1606.
However, it was not until the late 1700s that Europeans
began to learn more about this faraway place. Captain
James Cook sailed around Australia in the 1770s, and the
British started a colony for prisoners in 1778. This grew into
the great city of Sydney. A few explorers traveled around
the country's coast. However, until the middle of the 1800s,
no Europeans knew what lay beyond the coastline, where
all the settlements were. All they knew were the stories that
the native Australians, called *aborigines* (ab•uh•**rij**•uh•nees),

told. They described a dreadfully hot and dry desert that covered almost the entire continent. This part of the country is called the *Australian Outback*.

Charles Sturt Explores the Interior of Australia

In the early 1800s, Australia consisted of a line of coastal towns straggling southward from Sydney in the east around to Melbourne (**mel•buhrn**) and nearby Adelaide (**ad•uhl•ayd**) in the south. Fifty miles inland civilization ended. So little was known about the interior of Australia, it was referred to as the Ghastly Blank.

In 1844, a man named Charles Sturt struck out from Adelaide, Australia, in an attempt to reach the center of the continent. Many people believed that at the heart of the continent there was a great inland sea. This would make the interior just as inhabitable as the coast, and people were anxious to know more about it.

Sturt was so convinced they would find the inland waters that he took a boat along on the expedition so that they would have some way of exploring the mythical sea. The trip was long and hard. The desert was so hot that the ink Sturt used to take notes evaporated before it hit the paper and his thermometers burst from the heat. Many of his men got scurvy along the way, and Sturt's own health deteriorated from the difficult journey.

To his great disappointment, Sturt did not find an inland sea. He and his men found shallow salt lakes, deserts, and forbidding mountains. But the trip wasn't a total loss. They also observed prairies suitable for inland sheep raising, forests with valuable hardwood, and rivers that could be used to ship goods. The door to Australia's interior had been opened.

Burke and Wills Venture Into the Outback

In 1859, the government of an Australian state offered a prize to anyone who could travel the whole length of the country. Communication was difficult between the southern and northern coastal towns. The government was anxious to find a north-south route for a telegraph line. Robert Burke and William Wills were chosen for the expedition. They left the city of Melbourne in 1860 with great hopes and 25 camels.

Burke was chosen to be the leader, but he had little experience in exploration. Arguments quickly divided the party, and it split up at Cooper Creek, 870 miles northwest

Little was known about the stark conditions of the Outback.

of Melbourne. Burke ordered the rest of the group to stay at Cooper Creek for three months. He and Wills, along with two others, set off for the coast.

First, the weather was dry, and the group broiled in the hot sun. Then, rains came and the camels became bogged down in mud. Burke and Wills left the other two members of the group with the animals and continued on foot. Rats and stinging flies tortured the two explorers, but they eventually made it to the north coast in February of 1861.

They could hear the crashing of the waves on the shore, but swamps blocked their way. Burke and Wills were too weak to reach the sea. They returned to find their fellow explorers and reached the camp where they had left the animals. One man died along the way, but four days later, the three men crawled into Cooper Creek. They had been gone for 18 weeks.

Weak and hungry, the men were horrified at what they found. Cooper Creek was deserted! All that was left was a note to say the supply train had moved out only eight hours earlier, thinking they were dead. The men had no choice but to try to find their way back to Melbourne.

Both Burke and Wills died trying to make it back. The other man, almost insane with hunger and fear, was rescued by a group of aborigines. Although they died in the attempt, Burke and Wills are remembered as among the bravest explorers to challenge the Australian Outback.

John McDouall Stuart Makes It Out Alive

In 1861, just five months after Burke and Wills left on their fateful journey, another explorer, John McDouall Stuart, set out to claim the prize for traveling from southern

Australia to the northern coast. His plan was to avoid the desert as much as possible, in favor of land already occupied by sheep and cattle stations. Seven months later, he arrived. After a long journey home, John McDouall Stuart proved that it was possible to travel across the Australian interior and survive.

Even today, the Australian Outback can be a terrifying place. Towns like Alice Springs, in the center of the country, offer safety to travelers. Almost all Australians still live in coastal areas.

Exploring Australia

INDIAN
OCEAN

PACIFIC
OCEAN

AUSTRALIA • Alice Springs

Cooper
Creek

Sturt
Stony
Desert

Adelaide

Sydney

Melbourne

key

Stuart ——

Sturt ——

Burke ——
and Wills

Chapter 8

Into the Heart of Africa

The ancient Romans were probably the first European people to explore the interior, or non-coastal areas, of Africa. They traveled across the Sahara Desert and followed the Nile River. As you read in chapter 2, the great Arab explorer Ibn Battuta also spent many years exploring Africa's interior. In the 1400s, Portuguese sailors began to sail down and around the coast of the huge unknown continent, trying to find a sea route to India and China. However, the heart of Africa remained a great mystery.

Why did Africa remain unexplored for so long? One reason is the continent's geography. Most of Africa's important rivers are difficult to travel. Why? There are many high waterfalls and places with rapids, or rough water areas.

These barriers kept explorers from the "easy" routes into the interior they had used in North and South America.

Another reason was the trade of **enslaved** people. Some European traders set up bases on the west coast of Africa as places to purchase slaves. Africans brought other Africans to these bases. Often they were members of rival tribes captured in battle. The Europeans did not have to travel into the jungles to get the slaves.

A third reason why Africa remained unexplored for so long was the difficulty of traveling. The heat was intense, jungles were thick, diseases were common, wild animals were frightening, and native Africans were often unfriendly. For all these reasons, exploration of Africa began much later than the exploration of Asia, North America, and South America.

Mungo Park

Exploration of Africa got a big boost in 1788. In that year, British scientists formed the Africa Association. The next year, the association asked a young Scottish doctor, Mungo Park (**mung**•goh park), to explore the Niger River. This important river begins near the coast in what is today the country of Guinea (**gin**•ee), then flows 2,600 miles (4,200 kilometers) in a large curve. It reaches the southern edge of the Sahara Desert in Mali, flowing through the legendary city of Timbuktu. Then it turns south and empties into the Atlantic in present-day Nigeria. It is the main river of western Africa.

In Mungo Park's time, no one knew exactly where the Niger's mouth, or source, was. Park's plan was to follow another river, the Gambia (**gam**•bee•uh), upstream, then cross overland to the Niger. His trip turned out to be a lot longer than he expected.

Park was taken prisoner by a local tribal leader and only escaped after four months. Then, while making his way back to the coast, he was robbed of everything he had. He was left alone, with no horse, gun, or even clothes, 500 miles (800 kilometers) from the nearest European settlement!

Mungo Park trudged on, often in water up to his knees. He did find the majestic Niger River and determined that it flowed east, which many people doubted. Finally, 19 months after starting his trip, he stumbled into the British trading settlement on the Gambia River. When he returned to Britain, he wrote a best-selling book, *Travel in the Interior Districts of Africa*. However, Mungo Park was not the kind of man to sit quietly at home writing about his adventures. He returned to Africa in 1805. He planned to start at Timbuktu and follow the Niger to its mouth.

This trip ended in disaster. Park was impatient to begin, so he left for Timbuktu during the rainy season. By the time he reached the Niger, 29 of his men were already dead from disease. This loss left only a dozen. With a smaller crew, Park canoed down the river for almost 500 miles (800 kilometers). At a small waterfall and rapids, natives attacked him. Mungo Park died there.

In the 50 years following Mungo Park's death, explorers pushed further and further into the interior of Africa. Some started in Egypt, following the Nile River to its source, while others crossed the Sahara Desert. Still others traveled northward from the southern tip of the continent. Each made stunning discoveries and added to our knowledge of this mysterious continent.

In Search of the Source of the Nile

In the history of African exploration, two pairs of explorers stand out. The names of the pairs are forever linked. The more famous pair, Stanley and Livingstone, focused on southern Africa, while the other, Burton and Speke (speek), tried to find what people had been seeking for thousands of years. This great mystery was the source of the Nile. Remember Ptolemy, the Greek mapmaker? He wrote about the source of the Nile. Ptolemy thought there were two large lakes, which were near four great peaks he called the *Mountains of the Moon.* In the mid-1800s, explorers decided it was time to find out if these mountains, and the lakes, really existed.

The Nile River allows goods to be transported in Africa.

Burton and Speke

In 1857, the Royal Geographical Society in London chose two men to head the expedition. Sir Richard Burton was already a famous explorer, having journeyed in Africa, South America, and the Middle East. Burton spoke 29 languages! He was also known as being conceited and hard to get along with. His second-in-command was John Hanning Speke, an army captain and careful planner. Although they would later quarrel, their names became famous together.

Burton and Speke organized their trip on the island of Zanzibar (**zan**•zuh•bar), off the coast of the modern-day country of Tanzania in east Africa. **Missionaries** had told them about two majestic mountains in central Africa, along with two large lakes. Could this be the area that Ptolemy wrote about so long ago?

The party included about 130 porters, or native Africans, who carried equipment; 30 donkeys; and enough supplies for two years. Their destination was a lake called the *Sea of Ujiji* (oo•jee•jee). However, disease struck almost immediately. Both Burton and Speke fell ill with malaria, a deadly tropical illness carried by mosquitoes. Weakened with disease, it took them five months to reach the trading town of Tabora (tah•**bor**•ah), about 500 miles (800 kilometers) from the coast.

Here, the two had their first argument. Speke wanted to head north to investigate rumors of a large lake. Burton, however, preferred to press on with their original plan to head west. Burton, the leader, won the argument, and they went west. There they found the Sea of Ujiji, now called *Lake Tanganyika* (layk tan•guhn•**yee**•kuh). But once again, the men fell ill. Burton became paralyzed, while Speke was almost blind from an eye infection as well as deaf. A beetle had crawled into his ear!

The men's sicknesses caused a big problem. They were unable to travel to the northern end of the lake to explore a river there. Did it flow out of the Sea of Ujiji or into it? If it flowed out, was it the long-sought source of the mighty Nile? They never found out and had to return to Tabora, disappointed.

After resting at Tabora, Speke decided to investigate the northern lake. Burton stayed behind. The lake Speke found he named *Lake Victoria,* after the British queen. Lake Victoria is huge and today shared by Kenya, Tanzania, and Uganda. Although he did not explore it thoroughly, Speke was sure it was the source of the Nile. Because Burton was still too weak to travel, Speke returned to England. There, he broke a promise to Burton and revealed what they had found. Speke also took most of the credit. How do you think Burton felt about this?

As you probably guessed, Burton was furious. He was even angrier when, two years later, Speke was chosen to head another expedition. Its goal was to find out, once and for all, about the Nile's source. With James Grant as his assistant, Speke traveled to the northern tip of Lake Victoria. There he found a river, flowing out of the lake over a waterfall, heading north. He was certain he was standing where the great Nile began! Once again, however, he could not prove it.

Florence Baker

Most of the explorers you have read about were men. However, starting in the 1800s, women also began traveling to unexplored regions. Florence Baker traveled with Speke in their search for the Nile's source. She was the Hungarian-born wife of explorer Samuel Baker. Incredibly, he had found her in a slave auction in Bulgaria! He bought her, planning to give her freedom. Together they explored much of Africa.

When Speke returned to England a second time, a huge controversy broke out. Burton claimed that his former friend was wrong. In 1864, a meeting was called to hear each man's side of the story. But, on the day of the scheduled meeting, Speke was killed in a hunting accident. He never got to present his argument. Was it an accident? Did he kill himself, afraid to face Burton? It remains a mystery.

Stanley and Livingstone

At about the same time Burton, Speke, and Grant were in Africa, another man was becoming the best-known African explorer of all. The strange thing is that he never intended to become an explorer at all! His name was David Livingstone, and he was a Protestant missionary from Scotland. Livingstone first went to southern Africa to work as a missionary.

Once there, he became outraged by the growing slave trade. He spent his whole life trying to stamp it out. In his search for new missionary outposts, he became the first European to walk across the Kalahari (kah•luh•har•ee) Desert, now in Namibia (nuh•mib•ee•uh), South Africa, and Botswana (bot•swah•nuh). He also explored the Zambezi (zam•bee•zee) River and its awesome waterfall, which he named *Victoria Falls*. When Livingstone returned to England in 1856, he was a hero.

He made several more trips to Africa, both to explore and to work against the slave trade. In 1866, he traveled again to Africa. For three years, he explored, looking for the source of the Nile and trying to end the slave trade. The letters he sent back home became less and less frequent. Many people began to fear Livingstone was lost or even dead. All of the British attempts to find him failed. Then, in 1869, the publisher of the *New York Herald* newspaper asked his ace reporter, Henry Morton Stanley, to go on a search for the lost missionary and explorer.

Stanley wandered throughout eastern Africa for nine months. Because he was not an experienced explorer, things went badly. It was the rainy season, so most of his native porters left and many men died of disease or exhaustion. Some were killed in a local war, and Stanley barely escaped death. Then, he heard a rumor. In a village on the shores of Lake Tanganyika, there was an old, sick European.

Stanley raced to the village. Had he found the long-lost Livingstone? On November 10, 1871, villagers led him to the hut of the old man. With his party carrying the American flag, Stanley approached the old man and uttered the famous words: "Dr. Livingstone, I presume?"

It was Livingstone. However, although he was sick, he was not lost. He protested that he still had work to do in Africa. The two men traveled together around the lake for several weeks. Then they parted. Stanley went to England and told the story of his search.

"Dr. Livingstone, I presume?"

His book, *How I Found Livingstone,* was a great success. Stanley later returned to Africa, where he explored Africa's last great river, the Congo. Livingstone himself, worn out by a hard life, died in Africa the next year. His body was buried in London's Westminster Abbey, the only explorer honored in this way.

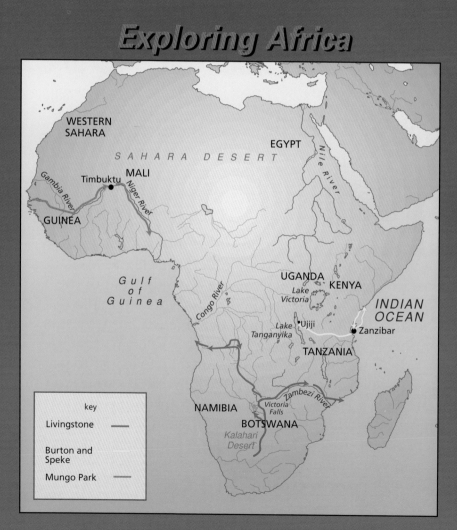

Exploring Africa

Chapter 9

The Race for the South Pole

Remember that globe or world map you looked at when you read the first chapter of this book? Well, look at it again. What do you see at the bottom of the map or globe? It's the smallest continent, Antarctica (ant•ark•ti•kuh). Try to think of some reasons why this continent was the last one explored. To start with, it's a long, long way from where most people live. Just to get there is a big adventure and a terrible risk. It's so far to the south that it is very cold. In fact, it's surrounded by ice almost everywhere. Once you get there, there's little to eat, there are no trees to build shelters, and there are no natives to help you. Put all these reasons together, and you've got one tough place to explore.

The closest continent to Antarctica is the southern tip of South America. Early sailors who passed this point, known as *Cape Horn,* came the closest to Antarctica. In the 1770s, Captain James Cook, the famous British sea explorer, became the first European to cross the Antarctic Circle. This imaginary line forms the boundary between warmer and colder climates in the southern half of the earth.

In the early 1800s, the people who came closest to the South Pole were sealers. They sailed on ships designed to trap large numbers of seals for their fur. Numerous seal ships came close to the coast of Antarctica, and they began to make maps of the coastline.

It might surprise you to learn that it wasn't easy to actually set foot on the continent of Antarctica. Why? It's so cold there that miles and miles of solid ice often surround the land. Explorers couldn't tell if they were on ice or on the land. It wasn't until the late 1830s that explorers finally could be sure they had discovered the continent.

The early 1900s began what is called the *Heroic Age* of Antarctica exploration. This is because of three great men who staged a thrilling—and deadly—race to the South Pole. Each wanted to be the person who first reached the southernmost place on Earth. The winner would claim greatness for himself and glory for his country.

Ernest Shackleton

One of these heroes was Englishman Ernest Shackleton. The Shackleton expedition sailed from England on August 7, 1907. After a brief stop in New Zealand, the party proceeded to Antarctica. They set up their tents on Ross Island in February of 1908. For the next three months, three of the crew members climbed *Mount Erebus* (**air•uh•buhs**), an active volcano on the island. At the end of the Arctic winter, in October, Shackleton and three companions set out for southern Antarctica. By early November, they had gone further south than any other expedition. They crossed into the central plateau of Antarctica on Christmas Day.

Shackleton and his group faced many hazards on their journey. By the time they had reached the plateau, all of their ponies had died and the men were running short on food. In early January of 1909, Shackleton and his party were forced to turn back. They were within 97 miles of the South Pole.

When he returned to England in June 1909, Shackleton was a hero. King Edward VII knighted him shortly thereafter. The Antarctic was now open for exploration. Although he failed to reach the South Pole, Shackleton had proved that it was possible to attempt—with the right organization, equipment, and leadership. Two men began what is known as the Race for the Pole. One man would win, while the other would die trying.

Scott and Amundsen Race for the Pole

One of the men was Robert Falcon Scott. This Englishman had already made a long trip to the Antarctic from 1901 to 1904 to gather scientific information. On June 1, 1910, Scott set off for Antarctica with 53 men, much scientific equipment, and ponies to pull their sleds. He promised not to stop until he stood at the South Pole.

A month later, a Norwegian explorer named Roald Amundsen (**ah•muhnd•suhn**) was about to set out for the

North Pole. When Amundsen heard that American Robert Peary (**peer**•ee) had already become the first to reach the North Pole, he changed his plans. His new destination— the South Pole. Amundsen sent Scott a telegram saying he was now trying to reach the South Pole, too. The race was on!

Amundsen's ship landed in Antarctica, and he set up a base camp at a place called the *Bay of Whales* on the coast of the Ross Sea. With four other men, 52 sled dogs, and four large sleds, he started for the Pole on October 19, 1911. The Norwegians dressed in Inuit-style clothing and traveled on skis where possible.

Scott's group also made its camp on the Ross Sea at McMurdo (muhk•**mur**•doh) Sound. Like Amundsen, Scott spent several months preparing for the trip to the Pole. Preparations included placing food and other supplies along the way. Finally, on October 24, 1911—five days later than Amundsen—Scott and 11 others set off for the South Pole. In addition to his ponies, Scott also used some sled dogs and the first motorized vehicles ever seen in Antarctica.

Right away, Scott ran into problems. New-fallen snow was very soft in the dry polar air, and the ponies had a terrible time walking through it. The motorized vehicles didn't work very well. Blizzards struck. When they reached the final resting point before heading to the Pole, all but Scott and four others turned back. The men would pull the sleds themselves, on skis.

After a week of hard travel, they were within 85 miles (137 kilometers) of the South Pole. In the journal he kept, Scott wrote, "I think it's going to be all right." Finally, on January 18, after 81 backbreaking days, Scott and his team reached the South Pole. Can you imagine how they felt when they saw, already flying at the spot, a Norwegian flag?

"It is a terrible disappointment," Scott wrote, "and I am very sorry for my loyal companions." Amundsen's party had made it to the South Pole a month earlier. Their trip from base camp was about 60 miles (97 kilometers) shorter than Scott's. Like the British, the Norwegians had suffered through blizzards. But their dogsleds could travel much faster than ponies or sleds pulled by humans.

Amundsen and his men spent a few days at the Pole, safe in tents. They left a sled and a tent, along with their nation's flag, at the Pole. In the tent was a list of the men who had been the first to visit this lonely spot. Then, they set off on the return journey. Thanks to adequate food supplies, they made it with no problems.

Scott's group sadly raised the British **Union Jack** next to the Norwegian flag. They took a photo of themselves.

Amundsen and his sled dogs

Then they began their return to base camp. In his journal, Scott called the trip "800 miles (1,287 kilometers) of solid dragging." The weather turned dangerously bad. They lost sight of the tracks they had used to journey to the Pole. Worst of all, food ran low and the men started to get frostbite. "Things are beginning to look a little serious," wrote their leader.

As the weather got colder and windier, the team's progress slowed down. The men grew weaker. On February 17, one of the men died. One night, another man, who believed he was slowing down the stronger members, made a decision. "I am just going outside and [I] may be some time," he announced. He did not return to the tent. On March 21, a

Scott and his expedition team

howling storm began that kept them in their tent for eight days. They were 11 miles (17 kilometers) from the next food supply.

In his journal, Robert Scott wrote these words, "We shall stick it out to the end, but we are getting weaker, of course, and the end cannot be far. It seems a pity, but I do not think I can write more." It was his last journal entry.

Exploring the South Pole

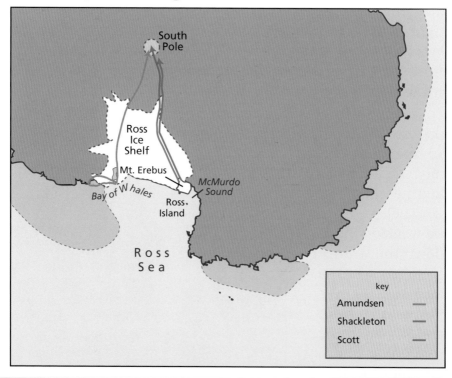

South Pole

Ross Ice Shelf

Mt. Erebus

Bay of Whales

McMurdo Sound

Ross Island

Ross Sea

key

Amundsen —

Shackleton —

Scott —

What About the North Pole?

Maybe you're wondering why this chapter is about Antarctica, or the South Pole only, and not about the North Pole, or the Arctic. The answer is that this is a book about land explorers, and the Arctic is not land. In fact, the entire North Pole area is ice. It's frozen solid most of the time, so it looks a little like snow-covered earth—but it's not!

The Arctic region was explored earlier than Antarctica because it was closer to where most people lived. Also, many Europeans sailed around the top of the world, looking for the Northwest Passage. In 1909, Robert Peary became the first explorer to reach the North Pole.

Chapter 10

Exploration Today and Tomorrow

Think about the way modern technology has changed the way you live. How would your life be different without things like computers, cell phones, radios, cars, airplanes, satellite communications, and digital technology for cameras and music? All of these technologies have greatly changed how explorers do their jobs.

When an early explorer like Ibn Battuta or David Livingstone traveled into an unknown part of the world, he lost all contact with other people. Today's explorers can usually remain in contact using satellite communications. When Scott and Amundsen sailed for Antarctica, beginning in the early 1900s, it took them months to reach their goal. With today's airplanes, polar explorers, and explorers of other regions as well, can fly to their destinations quickly. This saves much time and money.

Think about the Mountain Men of the American West or Mungo Park in Africa. How did they get from one place to another? They usually walked, while some rode slow pack animals. Today, tough four-wheel-drive vehicles can cross almost any desert, navigate almost any jungle, and climb almost any mountain.

As you can imagine, computers have had a huge impact on the way explorers work. The data found can be analyzed much more quickly with computers. Computers help make maps more detailed. Computerized instruments in the field help explorers and scientists collect much more accurate information.

A New Focus

The focus of the exploration of Earth has also changed. Because almost every place has been explored, the way we explore today is different. You might say that explorers of today try to better understand the places they have already explored. Think about it. An early explorer like Marco Polo traveled across the deserts of central Asia. However, he did not learn very much about how people, plants, and animals live there. He discovered little about what minerals lay beneath the land's surface, or how the environment of the regions had changed over time. Modern explorers are interested in all these things—and more.

Changes in Earth's environment over time is one focus of modern explorers. Visitors to fragile environments like tropical rain forests or mountain ice caps can use scientific techniques and instruments to measure these changes. Air and water pollution, global warming, and other changes can seriously affect how people, plants, and animals live.

What would you like to discover about our world?

Scientists and explorers of our time look for early warning signals of problems. The information they find helps other scientists make recommendations about how to solve the problems.

What will be the next stages of land exploration on our Earth? Certainly, using exploration as a means to solve problems concerning our environment will be important. Maybe you will lead the next expedition to the North and South Poles to keep a watch over the melting ice caps that have been a result of global warming. Maybe you will discover the secrets of the deserts and their hidden food supplies. Maybe you will be the one who can strike that vital balance between respecting the rain forests and utilizing their valuable resources. Or maybe you will find that the final frontier of Earth exploration may be right under your feet! Can you guess what it is? Earth's interior is almost unexplored, except for some caves and mines. What useful resources lie buried under the surface? What knowledge about how our planet came to be will be revealed? Only time, and the courage and determination of our world's future explorers, will tell.

Bibliography

Clark, William. *Explorers of the World*. Garden City, NY: Natural History Press, 1964.

Everett, Felicity, and Struan Reid. *The Usborne Book of Explorers*. London: Usborne, 1991.

Hale, John. *Age of Exploration*. New York: Time-Life, 1974.

Healey, Tim. *Explorers*. Morristown, NJ: Silver Burdett, 1980.

Keay, John. *History of World Exploration*. New York: Mallard Press/BDD, 1991.

Konstam, Angus. *Historical Atlas of Exploration*. New York: Checkmark Books, 2000.

Matthews, Rupert. *Eyewitness Books: Explorer*. New York: Knopf, 1991.

McCall, Edith. *Explorers in a New World*. Chicago: Children's Press, 1980.

Novaresio, Paolo. *The Explorers: From the Ancient World to the Present*. New York: Stewart, Tabori & Chang, 1996.

Saari, Peggy, and Daniel B. Baker. *Explorers & Discoverers: From Alexander the Great to Sally Ride*. New York: UXL, 1995.

You can also find more information about the earth and earth explorers at these Web sites:

www.historyoftheworld.com/explore/explore.htm
www.cybersleuth-kids.com/sleuth/History/Explorers/
http://edtech.kennesaw.edu/web/explorer.html
www.win.tue.nl/cs/fm/engels/discovery/
www.stemnet.nf.ca/CITE/explorer.htm

Web sites have been carefully researched for accuracy, content, and appropriateness. However, Web sites are subject to change. Internet usage should always be monitored.

Glossary

alpaca (al•pak•uh) a sheeplike animal of South America with long, soft, woolly hair

basin (bay•sin) all of the land drained by a river and the streams that flow into it

Buddhism (boo•diz•uhm) a religion based on the teachings of Buddha

caravans (kar•uh•vanz) large groups of traveling merchants and their goods

commodity (kuh•mod•i•tee) anything that is bought and sold

condor (kon•dor) a large vulture with a ruffled neck and bare head

continents (kon•tuh•nuhnts) very large landmasses

enslaved (en•slavd) made a slave

eternal (i•tur•nuhl) lasting forever

foretold (for•tohld) to have told or shown before

frontier (frun•teer) the borderline between known and unknown regions

habitats (hab•i•tats) the places where animals or plants naturally live and grow

intrigued (in•treegd) to have excited with interest or curiosity

latitude (lat•i•tood) location north and south

marauding (muh•rawd•ing) going in search of something to steal

missionaries (mish•uh•ner•eez) people sent on a religious mission

nomadic (noh•mad•ik) describes people who travel from place to place

pilgrimage (pil•gruh•mij) a journey to a sacred place

piranhas (pi•rahn•uhz) small South American freshwater fish having very sharp teeth

ransom (ran•suhm) a price demanded, before someone or something is set free

rebelled (ri•beld) to have resisted authority instead of obeying

treasuries (trezh•uh•reez) places where money is kept

tributaries (trib•yuh•ter•eez) streams or rivers that flow into larger bodies of water

Union Jack (yoon•yuhn jak) a flag consisting entirely of a union

vicuna (veye•koon•yuh) a wild mammal of South America related to a llama

Index